THE FORGOTTEN RULES OF PRAYER

K.C. Hairston

Limited Edition

The Forgotten Rules of Prayer
Limited Edition (Third Printing)
ISBN: 978-0-692-72508-5

10 09 08 07 06 / 6 5 4 3

Published in 2017

All scripture quotations, unless otherwise indicated, are taken from the HOLY BIBLE, NEW INTERNATIONAL VERSION®. NIV®. Copyright ©1973, 1978, 1984 by International Bible Society. Used by permission of Zondervan. All rights reserved.

Scripture quotations marked NAS are taken from the NEW AMERICAN STANDARD BIBLE ®, Copyright © 1960, 1962, 1963, 1968, 1971, 1972, 1973, 1975, 1977, 1995 by The Lockman Foundation. Used by permission.

Scripture quotations marked NLT are taken from the Holy Bible, New Living Translation, copyright © 1966. Used by permission of Tyndale House Publishers, Inc., Wheaton, Illinois 60189. All rights reserved.

Cataloging-in-Publication Data Available

For consistency, all pronouns of Jesus, God and Lord have been capitalized.

Printed in the United States of America

I dedicate this Limited Edition to Billy Graham, who reminded us that the three most important things we can do are to "pray, pray, pray."

ACKNOWLEDGMENTS

I would like to acknowledge Matt Denard, Rev. John Mount, and the members of Aldersgate United Methodist Church in Birmingham, Alabama for assisting me in the creation of this book. Thank you very much.

"Ask, and it shall be given to you; seek, and you shall find; knock, and it shall be opened to you. For everyone who asks receives, and he who seeks finds, and to him who knocks it shall be opened."

MATTHEW 7:7–8 (NAS)

CONTENTS

"There is nothing that two people can't do, if one of them is God."

– UNKNOWN

The basis on which God chooses to answer our prayers is a question that man simply cannot answer. However, by searching through the Bible and uncovering God's instructions for prayer, I believe we can maximize the likelihood that our prayers *will* be answered in the future. The exact manner in which prayer works is a secret, and that secret has not yet been revealed to us on earth. According to Deuteronomy 29:29, "The secret things belong to the Lord our God, but the things revealed belong to us and our children forever, that we may follow all the words of this law." In light of Deuteronomy 29:29, the goal of this book is to combine all of the cherished "revealed" rules on prayer and present them in a format that can be passed down, as was intended, from generation to generation.

The rules provided in this book were taken directly from God's Word—the Bible—and the writing of this book was premised on the following verse:

"I testify to everyone who hears the words of the prophecy of this book: if anyone adds to them, God shall add to him the plagues which are written in this book; and if anyone takes away from the words of the book of this prophecy, God shall take away his part of the tree of life and from the holy city, which are written in this book."

Revelation 22:18–19 (NAS)

Accordingly, careful attention has been given to ensure that nothing was added or taken away from the rules on prayer that God has revealed through the Bible.

HOW TO READ THIS BOOK

This book discusses 28 forgotten rules on prayer. After every fourth rule, an answered prayer from the Bible is included that illustrates the importance and use of the previous four rules. It is recommended that each time you read a portion of this book, you read a complete set of four rules and the following answered prayer. This approach is helpful to fully grasp the author's intent and will maximize your experience as you read *The Forgotten Rules of Prayer.* **Although this book presents 28 forgotten rules on prayer, it is not the author's intent to suggest that all 28 rules must be used every time we pray. The most important part of prayer is to do it, regardless of which rules are followed.**

What good is a rule if it is forgotten?

THE FORGOTTEN RULES

#1

ASK, DON'T DEMAND.

"If we ask anything according to His will, He hears us."

1 JOHN 5:14 (NAS)

The key to 1 John 5:14 is that we must ask, not demand, for God to answer our prayers. It is important to remember this rule when preparing our hearts and minds for prayer and when choosing how to word our prayers for God. Sometimes, the mere manner in which we word our prayers can determine whether they are a request or a demand. One of the best examples we have of following this forgotten rule is provided by Jesus Himself. The Bible tells us that Jesus used a similar method when praying to God. For example, we are told in Matthew 26:39, that just prior to His death, Jesus prayed, "My Father, if it is possible, may this cup be taken from Me. Yet not as I will, but as You will." Jesus chose to include in His prayer the phrase, "if it is possible," even though He knew that God had the power to do anything. It is clear that Jesus included this phrase in an effort to make His prayer a request, and not a demand. Jesus also included the phrase, "not as I will, but as You will." Both phrases allowed Jesus to present His prayers in the proper manner before God, and variations of these phrases can be used to help ensure that our own prayers are presented as requests and not demands. Similarly, the illustrative prayer that Jesus gave His disciples as an example of how to pray contained the phrase "Your kingdom come, *Your will be done* on earth as it is in heaven."[1] Like Jesus' own prayers and the example He gave His disciples, we too should word our prayers to ensure that they are not conveyed as demands, but as prayers to reveal God's will in our lives.

Of course, when we ask for God's will in a particular situation, there is always the likelihood that His desires will differ from ours. However, even when God chooses not to answer our prayers in the manner we request, it is still important that we prayed. This is because when God does not answer our prayers, He provides us the strength that we need to cope with His answer, and it becomes an opportunity for us to grow. In other words, sometimes God's will can only be obtained by not answering our prayers in the way that we desire, but in these situations He still provides us with the strength needed to accept His answer.

An example of this very situation occurred when God chose not to answer Jesus' prayer that He not be crucified. According to Luke 22:43, as Jesus was praying, "an angel from heaven appeared to Him and strengthened Him." In the same way, God will strengthen us when He chooses not to answer our prayers.

The bottom line is that, as servants of God, we have no right to demand that God act according to our will. Therefore, it is important to practice this rule in our prayers as we are instructed in 1 John 5:14, "If we ask for anything according to His will, He hears us." To increase the effectiveness of any prayer, we must *ask, not demand.*

#2

DON'T PUT GOD TO A TEST.

"You shall not put the Lord your God to the test."

DEUTERONOMY 6:16 (NAS)

Our prayers should not be used as a means to test God. According to the Bible, Jesus memorized Deuteronomy 6:16 and applied this rule in His own life. One day, Jesus was approached by the devil and was taken to the highest point of a temple. While standing at the top of the temple, the devil told Jesus to throw Himself down to see if God would send His angels to rescue Him. Rather than put God to such a test, Jesus quoted Deuteronomy 6:16 and stated, "It is also written: 'Do not put the Lord your God to the test.'"[2] The fact that Jesus took the time to memorize Deuteronomy 6:16 illustrates how important this rule is and serves as an example that we too should commit this verse to memory and apply it to our own communications with God.

After memorizing this rule, you will likely be surprised at how often it needs to be applied. We often unknowingly test God in order to assure ourselves of His presence in a situation. Applying this rule, however, begs the question: Is there a difference between testing God (which is forbidden) and asking God for a sign (which was commonly permitted in ancient times)? The answer is yes; there is a difference. To further answer this question, it is necessary to carefully examine the purpose behind each of our requests. For example, if our request is because we have a lack of faith in God's ability, then it is a *test* and is forbidden. On the other hand, if the purpose behind our request is to clarify God's purpose or to help interpret what God wants us to do, then we are requesting a *sign*, and such requests are permitted.

One example that helps illustrate the difference between a sign and a test can be found in Judges 6. In this chapter, God encouraged a man named Gideon to lead his army to save Israel from the mighty army of Midianites. The only problem was that Gideon's army was the weakest in the region and not the best army to select if you wanted to fight the well-trained Midianites. To clarify that God was really requesting Gideon to lead his army to fight the Midianites, Gideon made the following request to God: "If now I have found favor in Your eyes, give me a sign that it is really You talking to me."[3] Gideon then placed a sacrifice on an altar, and the Lord exploded the sacrifice into flames. When Gideon realized that God really was telling him to go and fight for Israel, he said "Ah, Sovereign Lord! I have seen the angel of the Lord face to face!"[4] Here God clarified His purpose for Gideon and granted Gideon's request for a sign. It is important to recognize that Gideon's request was not made to test the existence of God, but to clarify God's purpose. God's granting of such a request illustrates that it is not forbidden to ask for a sign if done for the right reasons. Therefore, to prevent our prayers from being hindered, we need to make sure *before* we pray that our prayers are not tests for God—although they can be for a clarification of God's purpose.

#3

BELIEVE IN THE POWER OF PRAYER.

"All things you ask in prayer, believing, you shall receive."

MARK 11:24 (NAS)

This point was made very clear one day when Jesus' followers witnessed Him command that a fig tree never bear fruit again. At this point, the tree withered up. Amazed, Jesus' followers asked how He was able to perform such an act. Jesus answered, "Truly I say to you, if you have faith, and do not doubt, you shall not only do what was done to the fig tree, but even if you say to this mountain, 'Be taken up and cast into the sea,' it shall happen. And all things you ask in prayer, *believing,* you shall receive."[5] By choosing this metaphor, Jesus showed how far our faith should go—and how powerful our faith can be. The question that sometimes needs to be asked is "What is your mountain?" By identifying the mountains in our own lives and having the proper faith, the mountains can be moved.

Biblical passages on prayer use the word "faith" synonymously with the term "believing." Regarding the term "faith," Hebrews 11:1–2 states, "Now faith is being sure of what we hope for and certain of what we do not see. This is what the ancients were commended for." Describing the importance of faith, James 1:6–7 states, "But he must ask in faith without any doubting, for the one who doubts is like the surf of the sea, driven and tossed by the wind. *For that man ought not to expect that he will receive anything from the Lord.*[6] According to James 1:6–7, if you ask while doubting the power of God, you should expect nothing from Him.

Despite the uncertainties of how prayer works, one aspect of powerful prayer is very clear: in order for our prayers to be effective, we must believe that what we are asking for can actually be granted no matter how improbable our request may be. In other words, we must approach God with confidence. Hebrews 4:16 states, "Let us then approach the throne of grace with confidence, so that we may receive mercy and find grace to help us in our time of need."

Because God is all knowing and is aware of our doubts, it is important to prepare mentally before praying. We must search for and resolve any doubts we have in God's ability to answer our prayers before we lay our requests before Him. A good question to ask ourselves in order to see if we are mentally ready to pray is whether we really believe our prayer can be answered. If the answer to this question is "no," should we expect God to answer it—when God sees that the prayer is coming from a person in doubt? Rather, we should resolve our doubts first, and then pray.

Having the necessary faith and believing in the power of prayer before you pray does affect the power of your prayer. As stated in Matthew 21:22, "If you believe, you will receive whatever you ask for in prayer."

#4

BE HUMBLE WHEN YOU PRAY.

"Because you humbled yourself before Me and tore your robes and wept in My presence, I have heard you, declares the Lord."

2 CHRONICLES 34:27

Humility is a central theme of the Bible. The Lord promises, "If My people, who are called by My name, will *humble themselves* and pray and seek My face and turn from their wicked ways, then I will hear from heaven and will forgive their sin and heal their land."[7] To ensure that we approach God with a humble spirit, it is important to conduct a "soul search" before going to God in prayer. While conducting this "soul search," we should examine our level of humility to determine if it is in line with a person who is about to approach his Master, Lord, and Creator. For example, it is very easy for us to casually approach God in prayer as we are driving in our cars or during points of our day when we have spare time. But we must remember we cannot just casually approach God like we do with everyone else. Rather, we must remember that it is really our God we are talking to, and accordingly we should humble ourselves before going to Him in prayer. James 4:10 states, "Humble yourselves before the Lord, and He will lift you up."

To illustrate this point, Jesus provided the following story:

"Two men went up into the temple to pray, one a Pharisee and the other a tax collector. The Pharisee stood and was praying this to himself, 'God, I thank You that I am not like other people: swindlers, unjust, adulterers, or even like this tax collector. I fast twice a week; I pay tithes of all that I get.'

But the tax collector, standing some distance away, was even unwilling to lift up his eyes to heaven, but was beating his breast, saying, 'God, be merciful to me, the sinner!'"

Jesus then stated:

"I tell you, this man went to his house justified rather than the other; for everyone who exalts himself will be humbled, but he who humbles himself will be exalted."[8]

This illustration Jesus provided shows that God wants us to come before Him with a humble spirit. Accordingly, in order to receive God's grace and have our prayers answered, we should be humble when we pray. James 4:6

states, "God opposes the proud but gives grace to the humble." The bottom line is this: When we humble ourselves before God, we allow God to rule and direct our lives as He sees fit. In other words, when we treat God as God, He can act as the Master of our lives and use us according to His will.

One method of showing humility that is commonly referred to in the Bible is getting on our knees before praying. It is very humbling to kneel before God. This is a simple act that we can do to help us mentally achieve the level of humbleness that is required. It is written in the Bible, "Therefore *humble yourselves* under the mighty hand of God, that He may exalt you at the proper time."[9] Finding humbleness before you pray sets the stage for God to do amazing things, and not finding humbleness sets the stage for God to create it!

PAST PRAYER THAT WORKED

#1

The Prayer of a Leper: Matthew 8:2

"Lord, if You are willing, You can make me clean."

According to the eighth chapter of Matthew, one day while Jesus was coming down from a mountainside, a man with leprosy came and knelt before Him and said, "Lord, if You are willing, You can make me clean." At this point, it is written, Jesus touched the man and said, "I am willing." Immediately, the man with leprosy was healed. It is important to analyze the manner and wording of the leper's request to determine what led Jesus to answer it.

Each of the first four forgotten rules outlined thus far in this book can be found in the leper's request. First, the leper carefully worded his request in a way so that he was asking, not demanding, something from Jesus **(Forgotten Rule #1: Ask, don't demand)**. The leper accomplished this by saying to Jesus "if You are willing." By using similar words in our own prayers, we too can ensure that we are not demanding something from Jesus, but requesting it in accordance with His will. After this *request* (not demand) was made, Jesus touched the leper and he was healed.

The second forgotten rule can also be found in the leper's request **(Forgotten Rule #2: Do not put God to a test)**. Because the leper believed in Jesus' power to heal him from leprosy, he was not testing Jesus' ability to "make him clean."

By looking at the wording of the leper's request, it is obvious that the leper also applied the third forgotten rule outlined in this book **(Forgotten Rule #3: Believe in the power of prayer)**. The leper stated, "Lord, if You are willing, You *can* make me clean." Here, it is clear the leper actually believed and had faith that Jesus could grant his request. As noted in Forgotten Rule #3, according to James 1:6–7, if you ask while doubting the power of God, you should expect nothing. The leper believed and his request was granted.

Lastly, the leper's request was also in accordance with the fourth forgotten rule **(Forgotten Rule #4: Be humble when you pray)**. As recorded in the eighth chapter of Matthew, the leper knelt before Jesus prior to making his request. This is a clear portrayal of the leper's humble spirit and humbleness before Jesus. The same level of humbleness should also be found in our own prayers.

As evidenced by the leper's answered request, the first four rules outlined in this book are needed to properly present our prayers to God. Forgetting just one of these first four rules (or the other rules outlined later) can result in unanswered prayer.

"Our prayers must mean something to us if they are to mean anything to God."

MALTIE D. BABCOCK

#5

BE PERSISTENT.

"Then Jesus told His disciples a parable to show them that they should always pray and not give up."

LUKE 18:1

The Bible clearly instructs that we are to be persistent in our prayers. This rule goes hand-in-hand with other forgotten rules that will be discussed later in this book; for example, the importance of patience and waiting on God's answer. Although we are instructed to wait on God's answer, we are not to wait and do nothing. Instead of resting on the fact that we have prayed once for something, we should continue in our prayers. In Luke 18:2–8, Jesus told the following story:

> *"In a certain town there was a judge who neither feared God nor cared about men. And there was a widow in that town who kept coming to him with the plea, 'Grant me justice against my adversary.' For some time he refused. But finally he said to himself, 'Even though I don't fear God or care about men, yet because this widow keeps bothering me, I will see that she gets justice, so that she won't eventually wear me out with her coming!'*
>
> *And the Lord said, 'Listen to what the unjust judge says. And will not God bring about justice for His chosen ones, who cry out to Him day and night? Will He keep putting them off? I tell you, He will see that they get justice, and quickly.'"*

Jesus also provided the following example:

> *"Suppose one of you has a friend, and goes to him at*

midnight and says, 'Friend, lend me three loaves; for a friend of mine has come to me from a journey, and I have nothing to set before him'; and from inside he answers and says, 'Do not bother me; the door has already been shut and my children and I are in bed; I cannot get up and give you anything.' I tell you, even though he will not get up and give him anything because he is his friend, yet because of his persistence he will get up and give him as much as he needs."[10]

Jesus then went on to state the now-familiar promise, "So I say to you, ask, and it will be given to you; seek, and you will find; knock, and it will be opened to you. For everyone who asks, receives; and he who seeks, finds; and to him who knocks, it shall be opened"[11]—but the key is that we are not to knock once and then stop; we are to persistently knock until God answers.

#6
BE SPECIFIC.

"For they suppose that they will be heard for their many words. So do not be like them; for your Father knows what you need, before you ask Him."

MATTHEW 6:7–8 (NAS)

Being specific in our prayers is important for several reasons. One reason is that the Bible instructs us to be few with our words when praying. In other words, don't babble your prayers to God. The second reason is that being specific adds more sincerity to our prayers. The following example illustrates this point: if you run into a friend at a store and you say "Let's get in touch with each other and maybe we can go to lunch one day," there is probably little chance that either person will take the offer seriously, and the offer will probably never be thought of again. On the other hand, if you run into a friend and say "I'll call you tomorrow at your work number, and maybe we can have lunch next Monday," this offer will probably be taken seriously by both people and followed up on at a later date. Put simply, being specific adds sincerity and indicates intent.

This forgotten rule applies to all aspects of our prayer. For example, when we thank God, we should thank Him for specific things; when we ask for forgiveness, we should ask for forgiveness for specific sins; when we praise God, we should praise Him for particular attributes; when we pray for others, we should pray for them by name and for specific reasons—and the list goes on and on.

In order to pray specifically, it is helpful to think before you pray, and if possible, to keep a prayer list. A prayer list will allow you to keep track of the details. As summarized in Ecclesiastes 5:2–3, "God is in heaven and you are on earth, so let your words be few. As a dream comes when there are many cares, so the speech of a fool when there are many words." Being specific is not only what God has requested us to do, but it also provides sincerity, indicates intent, and therefore adds power to our prayers.

#7

HUSBAND AND WIFE RULE.

"Husbands, in the same way be considerate as you live with your wives, and treat them with respect . . . and as heirs with you of the gracious gift of life, so that nothing will hinder your prayers."

1 PETER 3:7

According to the Husband and Wife Rule found in 1 Peter 3:7, a spouse's prayer can be hindered if his or her husband/wife relationship lacks respect and kindness.

In Ephesians 5:25, husbands are instructed to love their wives, just as Jesus loved the church and gave Himself up for the church. Similarly, Colossians 3:19 instructs husbands to love their wives and not be bitter against them. This is how God expects us to treat our spouses.

As noted in the biblical instructions on marriage, we should be considerate, loving, respectful, and not bitter. A husband/wife relationship that does not meet the standards set forth in the Bible, can result in hindered prayer. As a result, this area should be examined if we feel there is a breakdown in our communications with God.

#8

DON'T USE MEANINGLESS REPETITION.

"And when you are praying, do not use meaningless repetition."

MATTHEW 6:7 (NAS)

After discovering this forgotten rule, I began to notice how often it was violated—not only in my own prayers, but especially when people gather to pray in numbers, such as in churches or other large groups. For example, although the Lord's Prayer was provided by Jesus Christ *as an example* of how to pray, some churches have fallen into the habit of praying the "model" prayer repetitiously in every service. Because the Lord's Prayer is often prayed in a repetitious manner, there is a danger that people are merely saying the prayer and not thinking of the actual meaning behind every word—in other words, they are praying meaningless repetition. However, memorizing and applying this rule will reduce the risk next time a memorized prayer is prayed and will serve as a reminder that thought and meaning should always be put into such prayers. The Bible states, "You will seek Me and find Me, when you search for Me with all your heart."[12] Meaningless repetitions are not from the heart and do not make effective prayers.

To counter the risk of praying meaningless prayers, it is important to take a moment of silence and prepare your mind before praying. A moment of silence can be used in several ways to prepare and add meaning to our prayers. First, having a moment of silence allows us to think of what specific items need to be prayed for. Second, a moment of silence can be used to search the motives behind our requests. Third, this time of preparation can be a time to think of sins that need forgiveness. Fourth, this time can be used to think of any forgiveness that needs to be extended to others. Fifth, this time can be used to think of specific things to thank God for.

I have attended several church services where the preacher has provided a moment of silence before leading the congregation in prayer. This is a great way of encouraging the congregation as a whole to put thought and meaning behind their prayers, including the Lord's Prayer. Whether alone or in groups, it is always good to have a moment of silence before praying. Preparing in this way prior to going to God in prayer will help you avoid meaningless repetitious prayers—and by doing so, can increase the power of your prayers.

PAST PRAYER THAT WORKED

#2

The Prayer for a Child: 1 Samuel 1:1–19

"There was a certain man from Ramathaim, a Zuphite from the hill country of Ephraim, whose name was Elkanah. . . . He had two wives; one was called Hannah and the other Peninnah. Peninnah had children, but Hannah had none. Year after year this man went up from his town to worship and sacrifice to the Lord Almighty at Shiloh, where Hophni and Phinehas, the two sons of Eli, were priests of the Lord. Whenever the day came for Elkanah to sacrifice, he would give portions of the meat to his wife Peninnah and to all her sons and daughters. But to Hannah he gave a double portion because he loved her, and the Lord had closed her womb. And because the Lord had closed her womb, her rival kept provoking her in order to irritate her.

This went on year after year. Whenever Hannah went up to the house of the Lord, her rival provoked her till she wept and would not eat. Elkanah her husband would say to her, 'Hannah, why are you weeping? Why don't you eat? Why are you downhearted? Don't I mean more to you than ten sons?'

Once when they had finished eating and drinking in Shiloh, Hannah stood up. Now Eli the priest was sitting on a chair by the doorpost of the Lord's temple. In bitterness of soul Hannah wept much and prayed to the Lord. And she made a vow, saying, 'O Lord Almighty, if You will only look upon Your servant's misery and remember me, and not forget Your servant but give her a son, then I will give him to the Lord for all the days of his life, and no razor will ever be used on his head.'

As she kept on praying to the Lord, Eli observed her mouth. Hannah was praying in her heart, and her lips were moving but her voice was not heard. Eli thought she was drunk and said to her, 'How long will you keep on getting drunk? Get rid of your wine.' 'Not so, my lord,' Hannah replied, 'I am a woman who is deeply troubled. I have not been drinking wine or beer; I was pouring out my soul to the Lord.

Do not take your servant for a wicked woman; I have been praying here out of my great anguish and grief.'

Eli answered, 'Go in peace, and may the God of Israel grant you what you have asked of Him.' She said, 'May your servant find favor in your eyes.' Then she went her way and ate something, and her face was no longer downcast. Early the next morning they arose and worshiped before the Lord and then went back to their home at Ramah. Elkanah lay with Hannah his wife, and the Lord remembered her. So in the course of time Hannah conceived and gave birth to a son. She named him Samuel, saying, 'Because I asked the Lord for him.'"

Hannah's answered prayer illustrates the importance of several of the forgotten rules discussed in this book. First, Hannah prayed persistently **(Forgotten Rule #5: Be persistent)**. Year after year, Hannah's family made an annual trip to worship and pray in the sanctuary at Shiloh. At the sanctuary, Hannah would pray for a child. During these trips, Hannah was taunted by her husband's other wife for her barrenness. Specifically, the Bible states that "her rival provoked her till she wept and would not eat." Despite these years of anguish and torment, Hannah was persistent, and, in God's timing, she was blessed with a son. Why God made Hannah wait can only be speculated—because the Bible does not state why God delayed His answer. In Hannah's final prayer for a son, however, she did reach a point where she stated that if she were given a son, she would dedicate his complete life to God. Maybe this is the attitude God was waiting for. In the same way, God sometimes makes us wait for an answer until He has accomplished His entire purpose for granting our request—but during this time, like Hannah, we are to pray persistently and not give up.

Second, Hannah's prayer was very specific **(Forgotten Rule #6: Be specific)**. Hannah did not just ask God to grant her a child, she specifically asked that

God bless her with a son. Hannah also told God exactly what she would do with a son—she would give him to the service of God. Hannah did just as she had promised. While Samuel was still a toddler, Hannah took him back to the sanctuary in Shiloh, dedicated him to the service of God, and left him with Eli the priest. Hannah was specific in her prayers, and God honored them.

Third, the compassion, respect, and love that can be seen between Hannah and her husband, Elkanah, were also important because their marriage relationship had the ability to hinder the power of Hannah's prayer. According to the Bible, Elkanah was very generous, compassionate, and encouraging to his wife. This type of husband/wife relationship results in powerful prayer. As discussed in **Forgotten Rule #7: Husband and Wife Rule**, not having the proper husband/wife relationship can hinder the power of prayer.

Lastly, Hannah's prayer was also powerful because Hannah did not use meaningless repetition. Rather, the Bible states that Hannah was praying with her heart. The Bible goes on to state that her lips were moving, but no words were coming out of her mouth. Hannah herself referred to her prayer as "pouring" her soul out to the Lord. This is a perfect illustration of how all of our prayers should be—not thoughtless repetitions of memorized prayers, but prayers that are full of thought and pour from our souls **(Forgotten Rule #8: Don't use meaningless repetition)**. The Bible states that after she prayed, "the Lord remembered her" and gave her a child.

Understanding how these characteristics played an important role in the effectiveness of Hannah's prayer will help us apply the forgotten rules to our own prayers—which can ultimately increase the power and effectiveness of our communications with God.

"He who does not pray or call upon God in his hour of need, assuredly does not think of Him as God, nor does he give Him the honor that He is due."

UNKNOWN

#9

DON'T LET SELFISHNESS CREATE WRONG MOTIVES.

"When you ask, you do not receive, because you ask with wrong motives, that you may spend what you get on your pleasures."

JAMES 4:3

Prayer is a powerful privilege that should not be abused. According to James 4:3, if we have a prayer that goes unanswered, one possible reason could be the motive behind it. Therefore, we should always be conscious of our motives before we pray. It is written in the Bible that "the Lord searches every heart and understands every motive behind the thoughts."[13] Effective prayers are prayers made for the right reasons. Philippians 2:3 states, "Do nothing from selfishness or empty conceit, but with humility of mind regard one another as more important than yourselves."[14] Motives are an important aspect of our prayers and have a direct effect on God's willingness to answer them.

If there is a potential for wrong motives, sometimes it is helpful to first pray for God to assist you in having the right motives. After we are comfortable with our motives, it is only then that we should pray. As King David declared, "If I regard wickedness in my heart, the Lord will not hear."[15] Having the right motive is a must for powerful prayer.

#10
PRAY FOR YOUR ENEMIES.

"Love your enemies and pray for those who persecute you."

MATTHEW 5:44

In Matthew 5, Jesus explained why we are to love and pray for our enemies. Jesus stated that we are to treat our enemies no differently than we treat our friends—because that is what God does. By treating one's friends and enemies the same, a person can grow closer to God's challenge: "You are to be perfect, as your heavenly Father is perfect."[16] Jesus further explained that God causes the sun to rise on the evil and the good and that He sends the rain on the righteous and the unrighteous. Jesus posed the following question: "If you love those who love you, what reward do you have?"[17] Think about it.

In Luke 6:27–28, Jesus stated "Love your enemies, do good to those who hate you, bless those who curse you, pray for those who mistreat you." Not only did Jesus instruct us to love and pray for our enemies, He also carried out these instructions in His own life. Jesus even prayed for the people who betrayed Him the most—the people who tortured and ultimately killed Him. As Jesus was hanging on the cross, moments away from dying at the hands of His enemies, He prayed, "Father forgive them; for they do not know what they are doing."[18] Jesus repeatedly provided us with examples and clear instruction that we are to pray for our enemies. Praying for our enemies is an important element of powerful prayer; it adds an aspect of unselfishness, and it is needed to offer God a "complete prayer" according to His instructions.

#11
PRAY CONTINUOUSLY.

"Pray without ceasing."

1 THESSALONIANS 5:17 (NAS)

It is often tempting to only pray when we find ourselves in a time of need. As we are all aware, it is not uncommon for someone to go days, weeks, months, even years without praying. By doing so, we are only expecting God to be there for us when we need Him—expecting Him to answer our prayers after we have practically extinguished Him from our lives. The Bible is clear, however, that answered prayer is directly related to our closeness to God. James 4:8 states, "Draw near to God and He will draw near to you."[19] If we expect God to be close and hear our prayers during our times of need, according to James 4:8 we should draw near to Him during all periods of our lives, not just the low points. Similarly, God told Moses, "I will do the very thing you have asked, because I am pleased with you and I *know you by name*."[20] It is important for God to know us by name. One way to ensure this fact is to pray to God continuously.

In addition, at all times it is important that we *convey* our thoughts and needs to God. The Bible states "Be anxious for nothing, but in *everything by prayer* and supplication with thanksgiving *let your requests be made known to God*."[21] In other words, although Jesus is all knowing and knows our thoughts, needs, and desires, we should still convey our thoughts, needs, and desires to Him in prayer before they can be answered.

One of the great misconceptions about religion is the idea that because God is all knowing, and because He already knows our needs, God will adequately provide and there is no need to re-convey such requests to Him. However, the exact opposite is true. All requests should "be made known to God." No matter how simple or obvious our wants and needs may be, our instruction is clear—"everything by prayer."

Since discovering this rule, I have been amazed at how many times each day I neglected it—I often catch myself expecting God to provide in a situation without even praying for it! Put simply, one of the rules of prayer is to pray—even for the obvious things—during the good times, bad times, and even those in between.

#12
BE RIGHTEOUS.

"The prayer of a righteous man is powerful and effective."

JAMES 5:16

One way to increase the effectiveness of our prayers is to live our lives as God has instructed—be righteous. As discussed later in this book, having sin in our lives can annul the power of our prayers. According to Psalm 34:15, "The eyes of the Lord are on the righteous and His ears are attentive to their cry." The Bible further states in

Psalm 34:17, "the righteous cry out, and the Lord hears them; He delivers them from all their troubles." In other words, we know that the Lord hears the prayers of the righteous.

In Psalm 37:28, King David stated, "the Lord loves the just and will not forsake His faithful ones." In Psalm 37:25 King David further observed, "I was young and now I am old, yet I have never seen the righteous forsaken or their children begging for bread." Here, King David points out that God listens not only to the righteous, but also to their children. During David's life, he was fascinated by the difference in the way the Lord treated the righteous and the unrighteous. The Bible shows us that the righteous and their children will receive special attention from the Lord. As summarized by Psalm 1:6, "the Lord watches over the way of the righteous." Psalm 34:19 states "a righteous man may have many troubles, but the

Lord delivers him from them all." 1 John 3:22 states that we receive from God "anything we ask, because we obey His commands and do what pleases Him." Proverbs 15:8 states, "the prayer of the upright pleases Him." Proverbs 15:29 states, "the Lord is far from the wicked, but He hears the prayer of the righteous." These verses illustrate an important point: praying effectively is more than just saying the right words—it's also based upon who is praying them.

PAST PRAYER THAT WORKED

#3

The Prayer of Solomon: 1 Kings 3:5–13

"At Gibeon the Lord appeared to Solomon during the night in a dream, and God said, 'Ask for whatever you want Me to give you.' Solomon answered, 'You have shown great kindness to Your servant, my father David, because he was faithful to You and righteous and upright in heart. You have continued this great kindness to him and have given him a son to sit on his throne this very day.'

'Now, O Lord my God, You have made Your servant king in place of my father David. But I am only a little child and do not know how to carry out my duties. Your servant is here among the people You have chosen, a great people, too numerous to count or number. So give Your servant a discerning heart to govern Your people and to distinguish between

right and wrong. For who is able to govern this great people of Yours?'

The Lord was pleased that Solomon had asked for this. So God said to him, 'Since you have asked for this and not for long life or wealth for yourself, nor have asked for the death of your enemies but for discernment in administering justice, I will do what you have asked. I will give you a wise and discerning heart, so that there will never have been anyone like you, nor will there ever be. Moreover, I will give you what you have not asked for —both riches and honor—so that in your lifetime you will have no equal among kings.'"

The main theme behind this answered prayer is that we should not let selfishness create wrong motives. In answering Solomon's prayer, God stated that He was granting the prayer because of Solomon's unselfish spirit. As noted in **Forgotten Rule #9: Don't let selfishness create wrong motives**, James 4:3 states, "when you ask, you do not receive, because you ask with wrong motives." Here, just the opposite occurred—Solomon asked with the right motives and was given more than he requested. This prayer illustrates the importance of soul-searching before we pray to ensure that our prayer requests are premised on the right motives.

God also specifically stated in answering King Solomon's prayer that He was pleased because Solomon did not ask for the death of his enemies. As noted in **Forgotten Rule #10: Pray for your enemies**, Luke 6:27–28 tells us that Jesus Christ stated, "Love your enemies, do good to those who hate you, bless those who curse you, pray for those who mistreat you." When we pray, God does not want us to pray for the demise of our enemies, but for their protection—as seen in God's answer to King Solomon's prayer, negative attitudes toward our enemies can hinder God's willingness to answer. Rather, we should pray for them like we would a friend or family member. Praying for our enemies is not only required of us by God, but it also includes an unselfish aspect to our prayer, both of which add power to our communications with God.

This prayer also demonstrates the importance of praying continuously as discussed in **Forgotten Rule #11: Pray continuously**. Despite being someone who had everything and being at a high point in his life, Solomon still turned to God for further wisdom. Solomon, son of King David and Queen Bathsheba, enjoyed every possible luxury while growing up in the royal palace. Solomon's continued dedication to prayer resulted in him praying even during these good times, which enabled him to focus on others and not himself. God not only granted Solomon's prayers for others, but God also found ways to bless Solomon personally—even though Solomon did not ask for personal blessings. All of this occurred because Solomon was a man of continued prayer—praying during the good times and the bad.

The righteousness of Solomon and his desire to live the type of life God had instructed did not go unnoticed by God. The Bible states that Solomon specifically prayed that God would help him distinguish between right and wrong. As noted in **Forgotten Rule #12: Be righteous**, James 5:16 states "the prayer of a righteous man is powerful and effective." After Solomon's prayer, God stated, "if you walk in My ways and obey My statutes and commands . . . I will give you a long life."[22] Solomon's righteousness and his desire to be righteous resulted in powerful prayer. In the same way, our righteousness can strengthen our prayers.

The forgotten rules discussed above are necessary for powerful and effective prayer. These rules have been provided to us through God's Word, the Bible, and should be applied in our own communications with God—so like King Solomon, we too can achieve the full power of prayer.

"The greatest tragedy of life is not unanswered prayer, but unoffered prayer."

F.B. MEYER

#13
DON'T WORRY
—TRUST GOD.

"Therefore I tell you, do not worry about your life, what you will eat or drink; or about your body, what you will wear. Is not life more important than food, and the body more important than clothes? Look at the birds of the air; they do not sow or reap or store away in barns, and yet your heavenly Father feeds them. Are you not much more valuable than they? Who of you by worrying can add a single hour to his life?"

MATTHEW 6:25–27

These verses relate to an important aspect of some prayers—waiting. Prayer is often reserved by today's society for times of need, and such times naturally breed worry. Thus, it is important to rid ourselves of worry before we pray. In order to do this, we must *trust* that God is in control and that He knows our limits. According to 1 Corinthians 10:13, "God is faithful; He will not let you be tempted beyond what you can bear. But when you are tempted, He will also provide a way out so that you can stand up under it."

To increase the effectiveness of our prayers during times of need, and to avoid worrying, other forgotten rules from this book must come into play. For example, it is important that we pre-condition ourselves before we pray by supplementing our worries with faith and trust. As previously discussed in Forgotten Rule #3: "Believe in the power of prayer," the Bible instructs, "But he must ask in faith without any doubting."[23] However, not only are we to *ask* in faith, but we are also to *wait* in faith. Psalm 46:10 states "Be still, and know that I am God." In other words, God does not want us to worry, but to trust Him after we pray. When we pray, we are turning our concerns and problems over to God—and that is where we should leave them.

#14

GIVE THANKS (FOR THE GOOD AND THE BAD).

"Give thanks in all circumstances, for this is God's will for you in Christ Jesus."

1 THESSALONIANS 5:18

According to Psalm 92:1, "It is good to give thanks to the Lord."[24] A vital part of prayer is giving thanks to God "in all circumstances" (good or bad) that He allows to take place in our lives. Although it is easy to praise and thank God for the good, it can be difficult, and even awkward, to praise God for the bad. But, there is a reason to praise God for the bad. It is important to understand that God does have a purpose behind allowing the "bad" in our lives. James 1:2–4 says, "whenever trouble comes your way, let it be an opportunity for joy. For when your faith is tested, your endurance has a chance to grow. So let it grow, for when your endurance is fully developed, you will be strong in character and ready for *anything*!"[25] God puts trials in our lives to create opportunities for us to grow. By thanking God for these trials, we demonstrate to Him that we trust Him and understand that He has a higher purpose.

Colossians 4:2 instructs, "Devote yourself to prayer, being watchful and thankful." As the Bible instructs, we should not only be watchful for things to pray for, but we should also continually watch for things to be thankful for. Every day, we take for granted so many things that God has provided. God wants to be acknowledged as the provider of all the things we take for granted, and prayer is one of the best ways to let Him know.

In addition, as noted in Forgotten Rule #6, the Bible instructs us to be specific when we pray. In the same way, we should be specific in the things we thank God for. Being specific is not only what God wants, but it also adds sincerity to the thanks we give God. To offer God a "complete prayer," we should include specific thanksgiving. As stated in Philippians 4:6 "with thanksgiving, present your requests to God."

#15
INCLUDE PRAISE.

"Praise the Lord."

PSALM 106:1

Put simply, prayer is communication with God, our Master, our Creator; we are praying to Him as His followers, His servants, and His creation. Accordingly, when we approach God in prayer, He *expects* us to praise Him. As our Creator and Master, God has every right to be disappointed in us when we approach Him in prayer, and rather than praise Him, we bombard Him with additional requests. Although God wants to be gracious to us, we must still approach God as God and give Him more than just requests. God wants to hear more from us than our needs—He already knows them. For our prayers to be complete they must include several required items—one of these is praise.

When we praise God in our prayers, we should praise Him for specific attributes and for the specific things He has done in our lives. To truly accomplish this level of detail, it is important to think of specific areas to praise God for prior to going to Him in prayer. A great way to accomplish this task is to keep an ongoing journal of the things we have to praise God for. In addition, praise is *not* something we are to give God in our prayers on a periodic basis. Rather, we are instructed in the Bible to continually praise God. According to Hebrews 13:15, "Through Jesus, therefore, let us continually offer to God a sacrifice of praise." We are instructed to praise God in all that we do. Therefore, every prayer should include an element of praise. It should be as common as the "amen."

When we pray with the right attitude, we will automatically desire to praise God. As King David declared in Psalm 147:1, "How good it is to sing praises to our God, how pleasant and fitting to praise Him." For us, it should also be pleasant and fitting when we go to God in prayer with praise. In summary, it is important that we not overlook praising God each time we pray, in spite of the desire to convey our own needs.

#16

BE CAREFUL WHAT YOU PROMISE TO DO IN YOUR PRAYERS.

"When you make a vow to God, do not delay in fulfilling it. He has no pleasure in fools; fulfill your vow. It is better not to vow than to make a vow and not fulfill it."

ECCLESIASTES 5:4–5

We should not make empty promises in our prayers. In order to avoid this danger, careful thought should go into every promise we make to God. It is often tempting to promise God that we will do something for Him if He answers a particular request or meets a specific need for us. For example, we often pray that if God does X, we will do Y in return. According to Deuteronomy 23:21–23, "If you make a vow to the Lord your God, do not be slow to pay it, for the Lord your God will certainly demand it of you and you will be guilty of sin. But if you refrain from making a vow, you will not be guilty. Whatever your lips utter you must be sure to do, because you made your vow freely to the Lord your God with your own mouth."

The bottom line is that God expects us to do what we say. As Jesus instructed, "Let your 'yes' be 'yes' and your 'no,' 'no.'"[26] If we tell God we are going to do something, we should do it. Prayer is not a time to remove yourself from reality and make promises you know you cannot keep. Before making promises in our prayers, we should remind ourselves that our promises will be treated as vows to God that *should not* be broken! Similar to the importance of writing our prayer requests down before we pray, we should also write down the promises that we make to God after we pray. This will remind us of our vows to God—which is the first step to keeping them.

This forgotten rule dates back to before the life of Jesus Christ. It is recorded that in the 15th century B.C., Moses reminded the heads of the tribes of Israel, "This is what the Lord commands: When a man makes a vow to the Lord or takes an oath to obligate himself by a pledge, he must not break his word but must do *everything* he said."[27] We are permitted to make promises to God in our prayers, but we must fulfill them and fulfill them in a *timely* manner. The same rule was also instructed by Asaph, a friend of King David during the 10th century

B.C. and witness of the Ark of the Covenant: "Make vows to the Lord your God and fulfill them."[28]

This forgotten rule is important because it was given to us by God as a warning, and this warning should not be "forgotten"—but strictly followed in our prayer relationship with God. As noted above, Deuteronomy 23:21 warns us that delaying or failing to fulfill our promises to God is a sin. As discussed later, Isaiah 59:2 warns us, "Because of your sin, He has turned away and will not listen."[29] Accordingly, breaking our vows to God hinders the power of our prayer. So, when in doubt just remember: "It is better not to vow than to make a vow and not fulfill it."

PAST PRAYER THAT WORKED

#4

The Prayer of Jonah: Jonah 2:2–10

According to the Bible, thousands of years ago a man named Jonah was thrown overboard from a ship and swallowed by a whale. While struggling to escape, he prayed the following prayer:

"In my distress I called to the Lord, and He answered me. From the depths of the grave I called for help, and You listened to my cry. You hurled me into the deep, into the very heart of the seas, and the currents swirled about me; all Your waves and breakers swept over me. I said, 'I have been banished from Your sight; yet I will look again toward Your holy temple.' The engulfing waters threatened me, the deep surrounded me; seaweed was wrapped around my

head. To the roots of the mountains I sank down; the earth beneath barred me in forever. But You brought my life up from the pit, O Lord my God. When my life was ebbing away, I remembered You, Lord, and my prayer rose to You, to Your holy temple. Those who cling to worthless idols forfeit the grace that could be theirs. But I, with a song of thanksgiving, will sacrifice to You. What I have vowed I will make good. Salvation comes from the Lord."

After praying this prayer, it is written that "the Lord commanded the fish, and it vomited Jonah onto dry land."

Jonah began his prayer by assuring himself that God really did have the power to answer his cry for help. Jonah specifically envisioned, "in my distress I called to the Lord, and He answered me." Similarly, Jonah stated: "The engulfing waters threatened me, . . . seaweed was wrapped around my head. To the roots of the mountains I sank down; the earth beneath barred me in forever. But You brought my life up from the pit, O my Lord my God."

Despite being deep under the sea, wrapped in seaweed and in the belly of a whale, Jonah prayed as though there was absolutely no doubt that God would answer his prayer. Throughout his prayer, Jonah conveyed to God that he was not worried and that his prayer was based upon trust. In **Forgotten Rule #13: Don't worry—trust God**, it is noted that when we pray, we are turning our concerns over to God and, as Jonah's prayer illustrated, that is where we should leave them. Jonah's prayer is a prayer that acknowledges trust in the Lord. Like Jonah, to achieve powerful prayer, we should also convey our trust to God when we pray.

Jonah also used his prayer to convey his thanks to God. Although Jonah was stuck in a whale, he still had the desire to be thankful towards God. According to the Bible, Jonah prayed, "When my life was ebbing away, I remembered You, Lord, and my prayer rose to You, to

Your holy temple." Jonah acknowledged in his prayer that God placed him in the belly of a whale, but Jonah was not angry at the Lord. Instead, in the prayer for his life, Jonah took the time to tell God that he would offer a "song of thanksgiving." Jonah was thankful to God even for the bad. Similarly, we should include thanksgiving in our own prayers, for everything—the good and the bad. As noted in **Forgotten Rule #14: Give thanks (for the good and the bad)**, 1 Thessalonians 5:18 instructs us to "give thanks in all circumstances." This is exactly what Jonah did, and it added power to his prayer.

Jonah's prayer was also powerful because it was a prayer of praise. Throughout Jonah's prayer, he repeatedly praised God for His power and for being there during his time of need. Jonah knew that God was with him and could save him—and he praised God for it. Similarly, our prayers should also include an element of praise.

In **Forgotten Rule #15: Include praise**, it is noted that we are to praise God continually—which means in every prayer and for everything. Without praise, our prayers are not complete.

Lastly, Jonah also realized another important aspect of prayer—the importance of keeping the vows that we make to God. After envisioning God saving him, Jonah promised to offer God a sacrifice with a song of praise. Jonah recognized the seriousness of making this vow to God. So, directly after offering God his vow, Jonah stated "what I have vowed I will make good." In **Forgotten Rule #16: Be careful what you promise to do in your prayers**, it is noted that it is better not to make a vow than to make a vow and break it—to do so is a sin. Like Jonah, we should not make vows to God unless we are sure we have the confidence, power, and self-control to keep them.

"You can do more than pray after you have prayed, but you can never do more than pray until you have prayed."

UNKNOWN

#17
DON'T PRAY TO ANYONE BUT GOD.

"You shall have no other gods before Me."

EXODUS 20:3 (FIRST COMMANDMENT)

In order for our prayers to be answered, they must be directed towards the only one who can truly answer them: God. If this rule is not kept, then every other forgotten rule in this book is worthless. For example, it doesn't matter if we obey the Husband and Wife Rule, live righteously, repent, etc., unless such efforts are directed toward the one true existing God.

This does not mean that God will not hear our prayers if they are not directed toward Him. To the contrary, God does hear all of our prayers regardless of whom they are directed to. But according to Deuteronomy 6:14–15, "You shall not follow other gods, any of the gods of the people who surround you, for the Lord your God in the midst of you is a jealous God; otherwise the anger of the Lord your God will be kindled against you, and He will wipe you off the face of the earth."[30] In other words, God hears prayers prayed to idols, but such prayers anger Him, and He does not answer them. There is only one God and, therefore, only one deity that has the power to answer prayers. There is no other real alternative. In Ezekiel 14:3, God noted, "these men have set up idols in their hearts and put wicked stumbling blocks before their faces. Should I let them inquire of Me at all?" God is the necessary ingredient to all answered prayers—without Him prayers will go unanswered.

#18

THINK BEFORE YOU PRAY.

"Do not be quick with your mouth, do not be hasty in your heart to utter anything before God."

ECCLESIASTES 5:2

The lesson here is clear: God wants us to prepare *before* we pray. In preparing for our prayers, it is important that we take time to organize our thoughts so that we can approach God with a purpose focused on specific repentance, thanksgiving, forgiveness, praise, and the need for God in our lives. God does not want us to jump into praying and utter whatever comes to mind. Rather, God wants us to prepare and be specific as pointed out in Forgotten Rule #6, Be specific.

When preparing to pray, however, there will be times when we will not know what or how to pray. During these times of uncertainty, we can simply ask God to let us know how to pray. According to Romans 8:26, "In the same way, the Spirit helps us in our weakness. We do not know what we ought to pray for, but the Spirit Himself intercedes for us." Being able to call on the Holy Spirit when we are unsure how to pray is a powerful privilege and should not be forgotten during our times of need.

The Bible also instructs us that we should clear our minds from all distractions before going to God in prayer. According to 1 Peter 4:7, "The end of all things is near.

Therefore be clear minded and self-controlled so that you can pray." Prayer requires preparation, and thus you must "think before you pray." By preparing our minds and hearts and planning before we pray, our prayers will be more focused and in line with God's biblical instruction on prayer.

#19

FOR ADDITIONAL PRAYER POWER, ADD A PERSON.

"Again I say to you, that if two of you agree on earth about anything that they may ask, it shall be done for them by My Father who is in heaven. For where two or three have gathered in My name, I am there in their midst."

MATTHEW 18:19–20 (NAS)

When two or more people pray together, God is present. One of the biblical examples of this forgotten rule occurred at an Israelite festival. At the festival, Jesus' apostles gathered together to worship and pray after Jesus' death. At this point, the Bible gives a very vivid account of what happens when two or more people gather to pray in Jesus' name. The Bible states that when they came together in one place, "suddenly there came from heaven a noise like a violent rushing wind, and it filled the whole house where they were sitting . . . and they were all filled with the Holy Spirit."[31] This was the beginning of the first Christian church. Today, almost 2000 years later, some of us have forgotten that each time we gather together to pray and worship in church, God is there as well.

Likewise, God is also present when you pray with just one other person; which means there are three participating in your prayer—the third being God. The Bible states that a cord of three strands is not quickly torn apart. When people pray together, powerful prayer results. Jesus stated in Matthew 18:20, "For where two or three come together in My name, there am I with them." Jesus does not state that when two or three gather in His name He *may* be with them. Rather, He states that He *will* be with them.

Referring back to Forgotten Rule #11, Pray continuously, we noted that God told Moses that He would give Moses exactly what he asked for, because God was pleased with him and because *God knew Moses by name.* In other words, when we draw close to God, our prayer is more powerful. With this being said, it is easy to see why having God in our presence as we pray strengthens prayer. Thus, for additional prayer power, add a person.

#20

LISTEN TO THE NEEDS OF OTHERS, AND PRAY FOR THEM.

"Pray for each other."

JAMES 5:16

Not only should prayer be considered a method of conveying our own prayers to God, it should also be used to convey the needs of others. The Bible instructs us to listen to the needs of others and to pray for them. In Proverbs 21:13, the Bible goes so far as to say "If a man shuts his ears to the cry of the poor, he too will cry out and not be answered." In other words, if we do not listen to the needs of others, we should not expect God to answer our prayers. This is simply the Golden Rule. Surely, we should not think that God was excluding Himself when He provided us the instruction in Luke 6:31, "Do to others as you would have them do to you." Accordingly, we are to treat others the same way we want them (including God) to treat us. We are not to be hypocritical by turning our ears from the poor and then demanding that God listen to our needs.

After reading Proverbs 21:13, I began to have the conviction and belief that if I denied the request of someone in need, I was setting the stage for God to deny my requests. I carried this viewpoint for almost a year. Working in a metropolitan area, I was constantly encountering homeless people who were seeking a handout. Applying this rule, I gave handouts to anyone who asked, sometimes giving out over twenty dollars a day. After giving out such handouts for almost a year, however, I realized that I had interpreted the rule wrongly. The key to correctly understanding God's intent behind Proverbs 21:13 is by looking at the literal meaning of the verse itself. The rule states that we should "listen" to the needs of others. This point was made clear to me one day when I was speaking to a friend, and I was sharing with him my struggles of complying with the rule set out in Proverbs 21. My friend shared with me the following verse in Matthew 7:6, "do not throw your pearls before swine, or they will trample them under their feet, and turn and tear you to pieces."[32] By applying this verse to the homeless, I am not implying that you should never give to the needy. Rather, what this verse means is that requests by the needy should not always be granted. If the person is merely being lazy or it appears that the money is going towards an improper purpose, our prayers are not hindered by a decision not to give. In applying this correct interpretation, I am now more cautious and vigilant. Although I always "listen" to the needy, I am careful not to "cast my pearls before swine."

Using our prayers to pray for others adds an unselfish aspect to our prayers and as a result it strengthens them. Philippians 2:4 states, "each of you should look not only to your own interests, but also to the interests of others." Accordingly, we should not narrow the scope of our prayer to cover only our own needs, but should listen to and pray for the needs of others.

PAST PRAYER THAT WORKED

#5

The Prayer of Elijah: 1 Kings 18:25–39

"Elijah said to the prophets of Baal . . . 'Since there are so many of you. Call on the name of your god, but do not light the fire.' So they took the bull given them and prepared it. Then they called on the name of Baal from morning till noon. 'O Baal, answer us!' they shouted. But there was no response; no one answered. And they danced around the altar they had made. At noon Elijah began to taunt them. 'Shout louder!' he said. 'Surely he is a god! Perhaps he is deep in thought, or busy, or traveling. Maybe he is sleeping and must be awakened.' So they shouted louder and slashed themselves with swords and spears, as was their custom, until their blood flowed. Midday passed, and they continued their frantic prophesying until the time for the

evening sacrifice. But there was no response, no one answered, no one paid attention.

Then Elijah said to all the people, 'Come here to me.' They came to him, and he repaired the altar of the Lord, which was in ruins. Elijah took twelve stones, one for each of the tribes descended from Jacob, to whom the word of the Lord had come, saying, 'Your name shall be Israel.' With the stones he built an altar in the name of the Lord, and he dug a trench around it large enough to hold two seahs of seed. He arranged the wood, cut the bull into pieces and laid it on the wood. Then he said to them, 'Fill four large jars with water and pour it on the offering and on the wood.' 'Do it again,' he said, and they did it again. 'Do it a third time,' he ordered, and they did it the third time. The water ran down around the altar and even filled the trench. At the time of sacrifice, the prophet Elijah stepped forward and prayed:

'O Lord, God of Abraham, Isaac and Israel, let it be known today that You are God in Israel and that I am Your servant and have done all these things at Your command. Answer me, O Lord, answer me, so these people will know that You, O Lord, are God, and that You are turning their hearts back again.'

Then the fire of the Lord fell and burned up the sacrifice, the wood, the stones and the soil, and also licked up the water in the trench. When all the people saw this, they fell prostrate and cried, 'The Lord—He is God! The Lord—He is God!'"

This answered prayer is a perfect example to illustrate **Forgotten Rule #17**, **Don't pray to anyone but God**. In Forgotten Rule #17, we noted that prayers are a waste of time unless they are prayed to the one and only true God. As seen in the Baal prophets' prayers, they were worthless. The prophets of Baal prayed from morning till evening, but there was no answer. They shouted louder, but there was no answer. They slashed themselves with swords and spears, but there was still no answer. When they stopped praying to Baal and joined Elijah as he prayed to the one true God, the prayer was immediately answered. At this point, they realized that there was only one God, and their prayers to anyone else were a waste.

It is also evident that Elijah put a lot of thought into his prayer before praying to God. Elijah set the scene perfectly by having the Baal prophets pray to a god that he knew did not exist. Elijah knew that after their unsuccessful attempts to pray to the false god—Baal—they would pray the same prayer to the one true God, and their prayer would be answered. After their unsuccessful attempts, Elijah meticulously arranged the altar and even put water on the wood. In addition to arranging everything perfectly, Elijah had also planned and knew exactly what he wanted to pray. Elijah prayed precisely and specifically for God to light the fire so that the prophets of Baal would believe in the one true God. As noted in **Forgotten Rule #18, Think before you pray**, we are not to be quick with our mouth and utter our prayers hastily to God. To the contrary, Elijah was not quick with his prayer but carefully planned out the events leading up to the prayer as well as the wording of the prayer itself. As a result, it was an effective and powerful prayer, and God granted it.

Elijah's prayer with the Baal prophets also illustrates the power of praying with others. As discussed in **Forgotten Rule #19, For additional prayer power, add a person**, when we pray with others, God is in our midst. In the same way, God was present when the Baal prophets assisted Elijah in preparing the sacrifice and stood listening as Elijah led them in prayer. This is evidenced by God's immediate presence and answer. For example, right after they prayed, "the fire of the Lord fell" and burned up the altar that Elijah had built. From the immediacy and the manner of God's reply, there is no doubt that God was present when the Baal prophets and Elijah prayed. Similarly, God promises to be with us when we pray with others.

Lastly, as noted in **Forgotten Rule #20, Listen to the needs of others, and pray for them,** we are to pay attention to the needs of others and use our prayers to provide for their needs. This was Elijah's sole reason behind his prayer. Elijah's prayer was not for his own gain, but so that others could know the one true God. God loves it when we come to Him with an unselfish prayer, and one way to ensure that this element is in our prayers is to pray for others.

"Without prayer we cannot find God; prayer is the means by which we seek and find Him."

JOHANN ARNDT

#21
SOME PRAYERS REQUIRE FASTING.

"And Jesus rebuked him, and the demon came out of him, and the boy was cured at once. Then the disciples came to Jesus privately and said, 'Why could we not drive it out?' And He said to them 'Because of the littleness of your faith. . . . But this kind does not go out except by prayer and fasting.'"

MATTHEW 17:18–21 (NAS)

When fasting and prayer are combined, they make for

very effective communication with God. The question is why? While the Bible does not provide us with all of the explanations, one explanation is clear—fasting allows us to draw closer to God. As pointed out in Forgotten Rule #11 entitled "Pray continuously," the Bible states, "Draw near to God and He will draw near to you."[33] Through fasting we can create a closeness to God.

We are warned in the Bible that our appetites can be idols and can take the place of God in our lives. Hunger can often become the center of our focus. Philippians 3:18–20 states that when we focus on food, we are setting our minds on earthly things. The book of Proverbs also warns of the temptation of food. Specifically, Proverbs 23:1–3 states, "When you sit down to dine with a ruler, consider carefully what is before you, and put a knife to your throat, if you are a man of great appetite. Do not desire his delicacies, for it is deceptive food."[34] Proverbs 23 talks about the "desire" and "deception" of food, and as such, it has the ability to take our focus from God. In other words, our appetite can become an idol—the center of our attention—a substitute for God.

When we fast, hunger becomes a greater distraction and creates the opportunity for us to choose God over a heightened temptation. Therefore, when we fast, every moment that we resist the temptation to eat is a recurring sign that we have the power to choose God over all other earthly things. This is full dependency on God—at this point we are closest to God and our prayers are the most effective.

Another reason why fasting increases the effectiveness of our prayers is that it allows us to humble ourselves before God. In the Bible, King David talked about humbling himself through fasting. As noted in Forgotten Rule #4, entitled "Be humble when you pray," 2 Chronicles 34:27

states, "Because you humbled yourself before Me and tore your robes and wept in My presence, I *have heard you,* declares the Lord" (emphasis added). Fasting can be a humbling experience because we are forced to strip ourselves of one of our greatest earthly dependencies and surrender our full dependence to God.

Similar to a forgotten rule that is discussed later, regarding the importance of praying in private, the Bible also instructs us to fast in private. Matthew 6:16–18 states, "Whenever you fast, do not put on a gloomy face as the hypocrites *do*, for they neglect their appearance so that they will be noticed by men when they are fasting. Truly I say to you, they have their reward in full. But you, when you fast, anoint your head, and wash your face so that your fasting will not be noticed by men, but by your Father who is in secret; and your Father who sees *what is done* in secret will reward you."[35]

The ministry of Jesus Christ began by Him going *by Himself* into the desert for 40 days, and during this time we are told that He fasted. The Bible states after the 40 days and 40 nights, Jesus became hungry. At this point, Satan approached Jesus and tempted Him by saying, "If you are the Son of God, tell these stones to become bread."[36] But Jesus responded, "It is written: 'Man does not live on bread alone, but on every word that comes out of the mouth of God.'"

In the same way, when we fast, we are given the same opportunity to demonstrate that God is supreme in our lives and that our lives are not dependent upon food or other earthly things but upon the word of God. During these times our prayers are powerful and receive great attention from God.

#22

FORGIVE OTHERS; THERE SHOULD BE NO ANGER IN OUR PRAYERS.

"Therefore, if you are offering your gift at the altar and there remember that your brother has something against you, leave your gift there in front of the altar. First go and be reconciled to your brother; then come and offer your gift."

MATTHEW 5:23–24

Although our prayers today are usually not accompanied by altars and sacrifices, this passage points out that we are to reconcile our differences with others before approaching God. Similarly, in Mark 11:25–26, Jesus stated, "Whenever you stand praying, forgive, if you have anything against anyone, so that your Father who is in heaven will also forgive you your transgressions. But if you do not forgive, *neither* will your Father who is in heaven forgive your transgressions."[37] The significance of this forgotten rule can be summarized as follows: Jesus died for the sins of man, and all man has to do is ask for forgiveness from God, and his sins are forever forgiven. However, by failing to forgive just one person, the shield from our sins offered by Jesus is affected. As a result, sadly, many Christians take comfort in knowing that Jesus died for their sins but don't obtain the benefit because of their failure to forgive others.

The bottom line is that God will not forgive us unless we forgive others. As noted in the next Forgotten Rule #23: "Repent; sin can annul the authority of our prayers," if God has not forgiven our sins, and we come before God with sin in our lives, the power of our prayers is affected. In other words, failing to forgive others can ultimately annul the power of our prayers.

Jesus further instructed that we are to continually forgive others. Luke 17:4 states: "And if he sins against you seven times a day, and returns to you seven times seventy, saying 'I repent,' forgive him."[38] According to Jesus there never comes a point when we are not to forgive someone.

As summarized in the Bible in 1 Timothy 2:8, "I want men everywhere to lift up holy hands in prayer, without anger or disputing." Thus, Forgotten Rule #22 of this book is "Forgive others; there should be no anger in our prayers."

#23

REPENT, SIN CAN ANNUL THE AUTHORITY OF OUR PRAYERS.

"If I had cherished sin in my heart, the Lord would not have listened."

PSALM 66:18

According to Isaiah 59:2, "Because of your sin, God has turned away and will not listen anymore."[39] Because all people have sin in their lives, every person must ask God for forgiveness from their sins before addressing God in additional prayer. As elementary as it may seem, the "request for forgiveness" section of our prayers should be at the very beginning. The rationale behind this organization of prayer is that if sin keeps God from hearing our prayers, and we don't request forgiveness until the very end, then the entire prayer prior to asking for forgiveness may fall upon deaf ears. Thus, it is important to ask for forgiveness at the beginning of our prayers.

It is only natural that we want to prolong the repentance portion of our prayer until the very end. For example, in our daily encounters with other people, we seldom desire to approach someone with "bad news." Rather, we usually try to start a conversation off with something positive. It is important, however, to note that the forgiveness portion of our prayers is one that God looks forward to. To prove this seemingly outlandish point you must look to the fifteenth chapter of Luke. In Luke 15:7, Jesus

Himself stated, "I tell you that in the same way, there will be *more* joy in heaven over one sinner who repents than over ninety-nine righteous persons who need no repentance."[40] Accordingly, repentance is important and should not be forgotten.

John 9:31 states that "we know that God does not listen to sinners. He listens to the godly man who does His will." As a result, we should start all prayers with a request for forgiveness at the very beginning; not only because it enables God to hear the rest of our prayers but also because of the joy that it provides Him.

When asking for forgiveness, it is also important to be specific as discussed in Forgotten Rule #6, entitled "Be specific." Although it is often tempting to ask for forgiveness in general, the Bible is clear that God wants us to repent for sins specifically. Leviticus 5:5 states, "when anyone is guilty in any of these ways, he must confess in what way he has sinned." Similarly, Numbers 5:6–7 states, "when a man or woman wrongs another in any way and so is unfaithful to the Lord, that person is guilty and must confess the sin he has committed."

The Bible warns those who do not confess their sins: "He who conceals his sins does not prosper, but whoever confesses and renounces them finds mercy."[41] Our prayers are not as effective if we do not repent—sin creates a barrier between our prayers and God. To find God's mercy through prayer, we should repent of our sins.

24

PRAY FOR THOSE IN AUTHORITY.

"I urge, then, first of all, that requests, prayers, intercession and thanksgiving be made for everyone—for kings and all those in authority."

1 TIMOTHY 2:1–2

The apostle Paul noted in 1 Timothy 2 that praying for those in authority enables us to live a quiet and peaceful life. Today, it is still important that we pray for those in authority. The Bible further instructs that these prayers are to be specific (for specific authority figures, circumstances, etc.). There is a recent trend in churches to provide members with prayer sheets detailing the names of specific authority figures (i.e., senators, congressmen, members of local government, etc.). This is great because a church's congregation as a whole may not be sufficiently familiar with certain events to enable specific prayer.

Even when we are not aware of specific issues, it is still important to pray for God to watch over our authority figures and to pray for God to help them live righteous lives. One way to do this, as noted in the next forgotten rule, is to pray that God gives the authority figure the power to resist temptation. The Bible states in Proverbs 29:2, "When the righteous thrive, the people rejoice; but when the wicked rule, the people groan." Thus, according to the Bible, we should pray for the needs of authority figures and for God to give them the power to live righteous lives and resist temptation.

Because God wants us to pray for authority figures, it is important to pay attention and be watchful for those in authority—this gives watching the news and reading the paper a whole new purpose! As a result, if they fail, and we did not pray for them, we are partly to blame. God's instruction is clear: we are to pray for "all those in authority."

PAST PRAYER THAT WORKED

#6

King David's Prayers for Deliverance:
Psalms 35, 51, 138

While fleeing for his life from King Saul, the future King David prayed a number of prayers, several of which are recorded in the Bible in the Book of Psalms. Below are some key excerpts from David's prayers—all of which were collectively answered when God delivered David from King Saul and crowned him king.

Psalm 35:11–15 (Humility Through Fasting; Praying for Others)

Ruthless witnesses come forward;
they question me on things I know nothing about.

They repay me evil for good
  and leave me like one bereaved. Yet
when they were ill, I put on sackcloth
  and humbled myself with fasting.
When my prayers returned to me unanswered,
  I went about mourning as though for my friend or
  brother.
I bowed my head in grief as though weeping for my
  mother.
But when I stumbled they gathered in glee.

Psalm 51:9–12 (A Prayer for Forgiveness)

Hide Your face from my sins
  and blot out all my iniquity.
Create in me a pure heart, O God,
  and renew a steadfast spirit within me.
Do not cast me from Your presence
  or take Your Holy Spirit from me.
Restore to me the joy of Your salvation
  and grant me a willing spirit, to sustain me.

Psalm 138:4–5 (A Prayer for Those in Authority)

May all the kings of the earth praise You, O Lord,
when they hear the words of Your mouth.
May they sing of the ways of the Lord,
for the glory of the Lord is great.

As discussed in **Forgotten Rule #21, Some prayers require fasting**. Fasting is a unique technique that allows us to become more dependent on God and to humble ourselves before going to Him in prayer. As noted in Psalm 35:11–15, David understood that fasting added a new dimension to his prayers. David specifically realized that fasting could be used as a method of humbling himself before God. This same technique can be used in our own prayers to add power.

We know that David had enemies. In fact, several of David's prayers were used to ask for God's protection from the many people that were trying to kill him. One of David's many prayers for protection can be found in Psalm 102:7–8.

In this passage, David states "I lie awake; I have become like a bird alone on a roof. All day long my enemies taunt me; those who rail against me use my name as a curse." Despite David's many enemies and his fear of them, according to Psalm 35:13–14, David was able to forgive them and pray for them as though his enemies were a friend or a family member. According to Psalm 35, when David's prayers for his enemies went unanswered he grieved for them as he would grieve for his own mother. As noted in **Forgotten Rule #22: Forgive others; there should be no anger in our prayers**, having anger in our lives can annul the power of our prayers. The fact that David was repeatedly tormented by his enemies could have had a drastic effect on the power of his prayer. If David had allowed his enemies to anger him, the result could have been annulled prayer. To the contrary, David did not allow his enemies to weaken the power of his prayers. Like David, we too should not allow others to affect our prayer relationship with God. To avoid this danger, it is important to forgive others and not live with anger in our lives. David was able to do this, and powerful prayer resulted.

David's prayer in Psalm 51 notes that having sin in our lives creates a barrier between us and God. As pointed out in **Forgotten Rule #23, Repent; sin can annul the authority of our prayers**, sin can prevent God from hearing our prayers. David realized this important aspect of powerful prayer and as a result pleaded for God to create in him "a pure heart." Similarly, we too should ask God to grant us a pure heart and to forgive our sins, so that they do not create a barrier to our relationship with Him.

In Psalm 138:4–5, we see that David knew the importance of praying for those in authority. In this biblical passage, David prays for "all the kings of the earth." Specifically, David prays that they will know and praise

God and that they will know the ways of the Lord (i.e., live a righteous life). As discussed in **Forgotten Rule #24: Pray for those in authority**, the Bible instructs us to pray for our authority figures in order that we can have a better chance for a quiet and peaceful life. David followed this rule in his prayer, and in the end he was crowned king.

The forgotten rules described above played a vital role in the success of David's prayers. Like David, we should also realize the importance of these rules and apply them in our prayers.

"Avail yourself of the greatest privilege this side of heaven. Jesus Christ died to make this communion and communication with the Father possible."

BILLY GRAHAM (ON PRAYER)

#25

PRAY THAT GOD WILL HELP YOU RESIST TEMPTATION.

"Pray that you will not fall into temptation."

LUKE 22:40

According to 2 Peter 2:9, "the Lord knows how to rescue the godly from temptation."[42] As declared in Luke 22:40, God does have the power to rescue us from temptation, but we are instructed in the Bible to *pray* for such assistance. Similarly, Matthew 26:41 states, "watch and pray that you will not fall into temptation." When praying for God's help, we should not only pray in general for God to give us the power to resist temptation, but to the extent known, we should be specific in these types of requests. This means that if we have a particular temptation in our lives, or we know of a weakness that we might be exposed to in the future, we should specifically request for God to protect us from that particular temptation. Matthew 26:41 states that "the spirit is willing, but the body is weak."

The Bible warns us to "be of sober spirit, be on the alert. Your adversary, the devil, prowls around like a roaring lion, seeking someone to devour."[43] With that warning, however, the Bible instructs us to "be always on the watch, *and* pray that you may be able to escape all that is about to happen."[44] God expects us to acknowledge our temptations to Him and to pray for protection from them.

Following this forgotten rule can strengthen our ability to live a righteous life, which will ultimately result in more powerful prayer.

#26

DON'T PRAY SO THAT OTHERS MAY SEE YOU PRAYING.

"And when you pray, you are not to be like the hypocrites; for they love to stand and pray in the synagogues and on the street corners, so that they may be seen by men. Truly I say to you, they have their reward in full."

MATTHEW 6:5 (NAS)

In a way, it is unfortunate that in today's society this is

not a common problem. Because of the manner in which today's society views religion, prayers are usually not performed out loud to gain approval from our peers. As a result, most people don't pray out loud on street corners, in the office, in a restaurant, or in other public places. But for those that do in an effort to glorify themselves (instead of God), "they have received their reward in full." In synagogues and churches, however, the temptation is still somewhat present to pray in a manner so that others may see. In these situations, this forgotten rule should be applied.

According to Matthew 6:6, "when you pray, go into your room, close the door and pray to your Father, who is unseen. Then your Father, who sees what is done in secret, will reward you." Matthew 6:1 also provides the following warning, "*Beware* of practicing your righteousness before men to be noticed by them; otherwise you will have no reward with your Father who is in heaven."[45] The key here is to avoid praying in order to be *seen* by men.

This rule is not to be interpreted as prohibiting group prayers. Clearly, God loves group prayers. To this end, Matthew 18:19–20 states that where two or more people gather in God's name, He is there also. Rather, this rule was given as a warning for prayers given in public that the focus should be on God and not on others in the group.

In accordance with this rule, Jesus often prayed in secret places. An example of this rule was illustrated by Jesus in the Garden of Gethsemane just prior to His crucifixion on the cross. According to Matthew 26:36, Jesus told his disciples, "Sit here while I go over there and pray." It was away from His disciples that He "fell with His face to the ground" and was able to truly humble Himself before God. Like Jesus, we too should place the focus of our prayers on God, and not others.

#27

PRAY IN THE NAME OF JESUS.

"I will do whatever you ask in My name, so that the Son may bring glory to the Father. You may ask Me for anything in My name, and I will do it."

JOHN 14:13–14

Usually, this is literally done by adding the phrase "in Jesus' name" at the end of a prayer. During His time on earth, Jesus repeatedly emphasized the importance of praying in His name. As seen in John 16:23, Jesus stated that we are to make our requests in His name. According to John 16:23, Jesus stated, "I tell you the truth, My Father will give you whatever you ask in My name." It should be noted, however, that praying in Jesus' name is not accomplished by merely stating it at the end of our prayers. Rather, the proper attitude and heart must accompany our prayers to offer them in Jesus' name. Our attitude and heart should be based on the foundation that Jesus is our Savior and that He died for our sins so that we can have a pure relationship with God. It is based on this truth that we are able to strengthen the effectiveness of our prayers by praying through someone who is sinless, holy, and whose relationship bears no hindrance with God.

Since God has allowed us the ability to go through His Son, we deny ourselves the ultimate power of prayer when we fail to follow this important rule. Forgetting to add this essential element to each prayer unquestionably prevents us from attaining the full power of prayer.

#28
BE PATIENT.

"Rest in the Lord and wait patiently for Him."

PSALM 37:7 (NAS)

According to Lamentations 3:25, "The Lord is good to those who wait for Him."[46] However, practicing such patience at times requires great endurance. This is because asking for God's hand in needful situations may involve us waiting for His answer. There is an old saying that the Lord will not give us more than we can handle. This is so true and great to remember in tough situations.

Isaiah 40:31 states, "Yet those who *wait* for the Lord will gain new strength; they will mount up with wings like eagles, they will run and not get tired, they will walk and not become weary."[47] Further instruction for situations that require patience can be found in Psalm 27:14 which states, "Wait for the Lord; Be strong and let your heart take courage; Yes, wait for the Lord."[48]

Unfortunately, there is no set time frame (at least that we on earth are aware of) in which God answers prayers. But we must always assume that God's delay is for a particular purpose—even if it is to build perseverance. In order to accomplish God's purpose, however, we must be patient and wait for His answer knowing that any delay is for a reason.

In summary, sometimes God's purpose cannot be accomplished by answering our prayers immediately, and sometimes the very situation that we are praying for God to take us from is one in which He intended us to be in. Moreover, sometimes it is tempting to feel that no action on the part of God equates to God not being in control of the situation. But knowing that God can have a reason for delaying an answer to our prayers can be exciting when we realize that there is a greater purpose. As God states in Isaiah 49:23, "those who hopefully wait for Me will not be put to shame."[49]

PAST PRAYER THAT WORKED

#7

Jesus' Prayer For Life: Luke 22:39–42

"Jesus went out as usual to the Mount of Olives, and His disciples followed Him. On reaching the place, He said to them, 'Pray that you will not fall into temptation.' He withdrew about a stone's throw beyond them, knelt down and prayed, 'Father, if You are willing, take this cup from Me; yet not My will, but Yours be done.'"

Just prior to praying for God to spare Him from death on the cross, Jesus found it necessary to instruct His disciples to pray that they not fall into temptation. Knowing that the disciples were about to face a time when prayer would be greatly needed, perhaps Jesus believed that

Satan would attempt to diminish the power of the disciples' prayers through temptation. As discussed in **Forgotten Rule #25: Pray that God will help you resist temptation**, God knows how to rescue us from temptation, but He expects us to ask for it. Jesus knew of the dangers of temptation, its effect on prayer, and the importance of asking for God's protection in this area. Likewise, we too should pray for God's protection from temptation—especially when we know we are about to face a time of increased prayer.

This prayer also illustrates the importance of not praying so that others may see you. As pointed out in Luke 22, Jesus "withdrew" from His disciples before He prayed. As discussed in **Forgotten Rule #26: Don't pray so that others may see you praying**, we are not to pray to be seen by men. Rather, our focus is to be solely on God. Like Jesus, we should make sure that our prayers are not an act for others, but are conducted only for an audience of one—God.

It is also important to note that the power of Jesus' prayer can be attributed to the fact that it was prayed by someone who had no hindrances in His relationship with God. Although we cannot achieve this pure, unhindered communication with God on our own, as discussed in **Forgotten Rule #27: Pray in the name of Jesus**, we can pray in Jesus' name to accomplish this same result. In John 16:23, we are reminded that God will give us whatever we ask for in Jesus' name (that is in accordance with God's will). We have been granted the unbelievable privilege of praying to God through Jesus, thereby utilizing His perfection to strengthen our prayers. Accordingly, every prayer should make use of this privilege and be offered to God in the name of Jesus Christ.

After praying the prayer in Luke 22, Jesus also showed the importance of patience. Jesus trusted in God and knew that no matter what the answer was to His prayer, God had a greater purpose. Jesus waited patiently for God's answer, and although He was crucified on the cross, He was resurrected in the end and ascended into heaven to sit on the throne with God. Jesus' death ultimately opened the door for believers on earth to attain salvation and eternal life. God knew of this higher purpose, and Jesus' patience allowed this purpose to be obtained. As noted in **Forgotten Rule #28: Be patient**, God has instructed us that those who wait hopefully in Him "will not be put to shame." Waiting patiently for God's answer is a key aspect of successful prayer—it is all about God's timing, not ours. Sometimes, it is only by waiting that we can fully receive God's answer. Thus, it is important when we pray to not expect an immediate answer, but to prepare ourselves to wait for as long as it takes for God to answer according to His perfect timing.

"I am the Lord, the God of all mankind.

Is anything too hard for Me?"

GOD (JEREMIAH 32:27)

CONCLUSION

The Bible has revealed to us what is necessary in order to effectively pray to God. According to the Bible, there are certain rules that we need to follow in order to achieve the fully intended power of prayer. Sadly, over time, several of these rules have been forgotten. The intent of this book is to compile the rules on prayer revealed throughout the Bible and preserve them in a single place. In all, this book reveals 28 forgotten rules on prayer and illustrates how each rule has been used in the Bible to achieve the full power of prayer. Near the end of Jesus' life, one of His apostles asked Jesus how to pray. As an *example* of how to pray, Jesus provided a model prayer for His disciples and all future generations to follow. This model prayer is commonly referred to as the "Lord's Prayer." The model prayer, which can be found in Matthew 6:9–13, goes as follows:

Our Father in heaven,

hallowed be Your name,

Your kingdom come,

Your will be done

on earth as it is in heaven.

Give us today our daily bread.

Forgive us our debts,

as we also have forgiven our debtors.

And lead us not into temptation,

but deliver us from the evil one,

for Yours is the kingdom and the power
and the glory forever. Amen.

Each forgotten rule of prayer provided in this book can be found in Jesus' model prayer or in the specific instructions that Jesus gave to the same disciples. By following these rules, we can all maximize our communications with God. Through all situations, however, always remember:

"The Lord longs to be gracious to you, and therefore He waits on high to have compassion on you."

Isaiah 30:18 (NAS)

PRAYER MAP

PRE-PRAYER CHECKLIST:

- Remove all doubts of God's power before praying (Rule 3): We must believe in the power of prayer. "All things you ask in prayer, believing, you will receive." Matthew 21:22 (NAS).

- Humble yourself (Rule 4): We must go before God in a humble manner. Although this does not mean that we have to get on our knees before we pray, sometimes this is a great tool to truly convey our humbleness to God. "Because you have humbled yourself before Me and tore your robes and wept in My presence, I have heard you, declares the Lord." 2 Chronicles 34:27.

- Be specific (Rule 6): Keeping a prayer journal helps us keep up with the details. "God is in heaven and you are on earth, so let your words be few. As a dream comes when there are many cares, so the speech of a fool when there are many words." Ecclesiastes 5:2–3.

- Importance of the husband/wife relationship (Rule 7): "Husbands, in the same way be considerate as you live with your wives, and treat them with respect . . . and as heirs with you of the gracious gift of life, so that nothing will hinder your prayers." 1 Peter 3:7.

- Pray continuously (Rule 11): Don't save the power of prayer only for disastrous situations. Pray during the good and the bad times. "Pray without ceasing." 1 Thessalonians 5:17 (NAS).

- Live a righteous life (Rule 12): "The prayer of a righteous man is powerful and effective." James 5:16.

- Think before you pray (Rule 18): "Do not be quick with your mouth, do not be hasty in your heart to utter anything to God." Ecclesiastes 5:2.

- For additional power, add a person (Rule 19): "Again I say to you, that if two of you agree on earth about anything that they may ask, it shall be done for them by My Father who is in heaven. For where two or three have gathered in My name, I am there in their midst." Matthew 18:19–20 (NAS).

- Listen to the needs of others and pray for them (Rule 20): "If a man shuts his ears to the cry of the poor, he too will cry out and not be answered." Proverbs 21:13.

- Some prayers may require fasting (Rule 21):

Regarding certain types of prayers, Jesus specifically noted "But this kind does not go out except by prayer and fasting." Matthew 17:21 (NAS).

- Forgive others (Rule 22): There should be no anger in our prayers. "Whenever you stand praying, forgive, if you have anything against anyone, so that your Father who is in heaven will also forgive you." Mark 11:25 (NAS).

- Find the right place to pray (Rule 26): Don't pray so that others may see you praying. "When you pray, you are not to be like the hypocrites; for they love to stand and pray in the synagogues and on the street corners, so that they may be seen by men. Truly I say to you, they have their reward in full." Matthew 6:5 (NAS).

PRAYER CHECKLIST:

- Ask, don't demand (Rule 1): "If we ask anything according to His will, He hears us." 1 John 5:14.

- Don't put God to the test (Rule 2): "Do not put the Lord your God to the test." Luke 4:12.

- Don't use meaningless repetition (Rule 8): "And when you are praying, do not use meaningless repetition." Matthew 6:7 (NAS).

- Don't let selfishness create wrong motives (Rule 9): "When you ask, you do not receive, because you ask with wrong motives." James 4:3.

- Pray for your enemies (Rule 10): "Love your enemies, and pray for those who persecute you." Matthew 5:44.

- Give thanks (Rule 14): "Give thanks in all circumstances, for this is God's will for you in Christ Jesus." 1 Thessalonians 5:18.

- Include praise (Rule 15): "Praise the Lord." Psalm 106:1.

- Be careful what you promise to do in your prayers (Rule 16): "When you make a vow to God, do not delay in fulfilling it. He has no pleasure in fools; fulfill your vow. It is better not to vow than to make a vow and not fulfill it." Ecclesiastes 5:4–5.

- Don't pray to anyone but God (Rule 17): "You shall have no other gods before Me." Exodus 20:3.

- Repent; sin can annul the authority of our prayers (Rule 23): "If I had cherished sin in my heart, the Lord would not have listened." Psalm 66:18.

- Pray for those in authority (Rule 24): "I urge, then, first of all, that requests, prayers, intercession and thanksgiving be made for everyone—for kings and all those in authority." 1 Timothy 2:1–2.

- Pray that God will help you resist temptation (Rule 25): "Pray that you will not fall into temptation." Luke 22:40.

- Pray in the name of Jesus (Rule 27): Jesus stated, "I tell you the truth, My Father will give you whatever you ask in My name." John 16:23.

POST-PRAYER CHECKLIST:

- Be persistent (Rule 5): Although we are instructed to wait patiently in the Lord, this does not mean that we should pray once and then stop praying. "Yet because of his persistence he will get up and give him as much as he needs." Luke 11:8 (NAS).

- Don't worry (Rule 13): "Therefore I tell you, do not worry about your life, what you will eat or drink; or about your body, what you will wear. Is not life more important than food, and the body more important than clothes? Look at the birds of the air; they do not sow or reap or store away in barns, and yet your heavenly Father feeds them. Are you not much more valuable than they? Who of you by worrying can add a single hour to his life?" Matthew 6:25–27.

- Be patient (Rule 28): "Rest in the Lord and wait patiently for Him." Psalm 37:7 (NAS).